MUMBAI
MASTi

KRSNA MEHTA
BACHI KARKARIA

To Kahaan, the Inheritor
BACHI KARKARIA

To my parents, for recognising
and acknowledging my talent
KRSNA MEHTA

ISBN 81-7508-510-X
© India Book House, 2007

VISUAL DIRECTOR Krsna Mehta
GRAPHIC DESIGN anirudh + vinay, Shweta Bandekar
PHOTO RESEARCH Aradhana Nagpal
EDITOR Nandini Bhaskaran
PROCESSING Reproscan
PRINTING Jak Printers

PUBLISHED BY
INDIA BOOK HOUSE PVT LTD
501 Mahalaxmi Chambers
22 Bhulabhai Desai Road
Mumbai 400 026
Tel +91 22 23523827
Fax +91 22 23538406
E-mail info@ibhpublishing.com

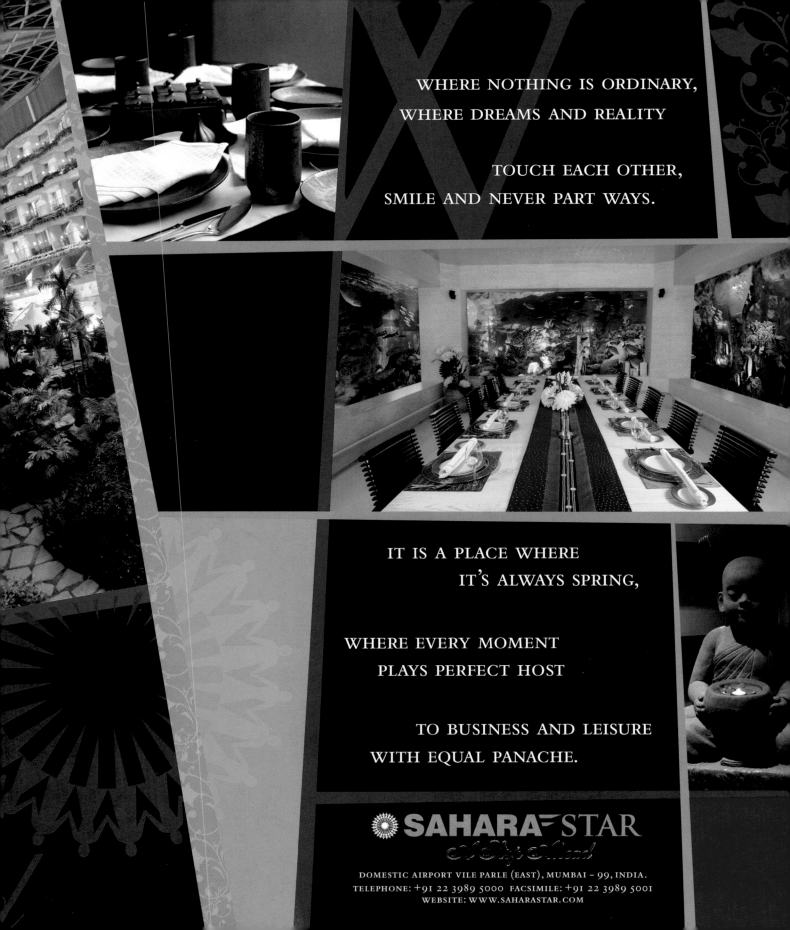

Mumbai Unzipped

Masti, Seriously

16

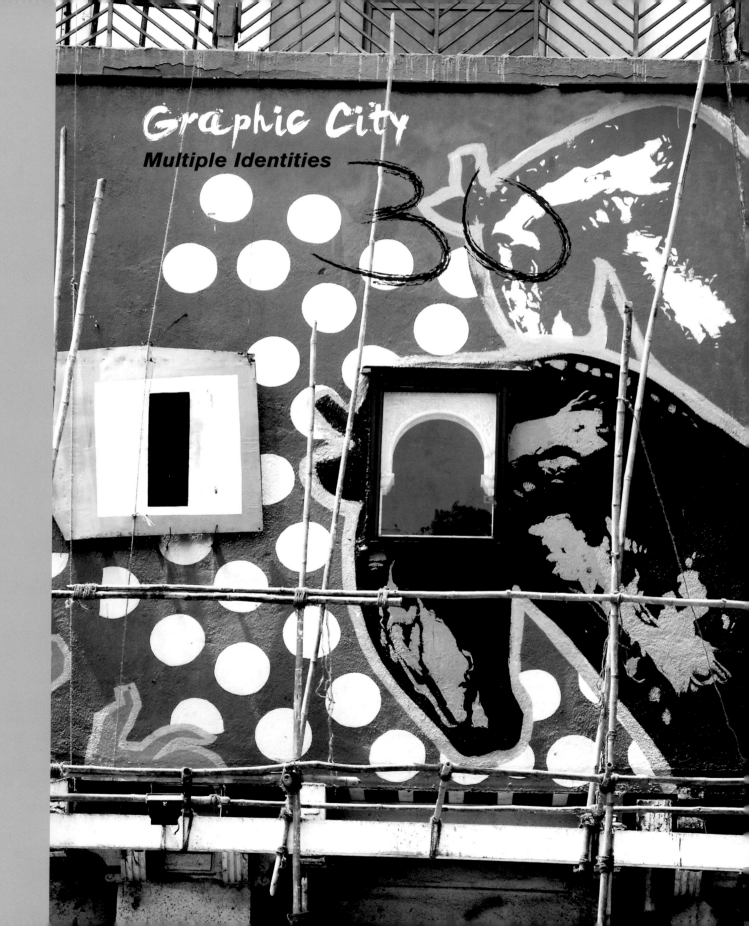

Graphic City

Multiple Identities

The Way We Are

A Living on the Street

42

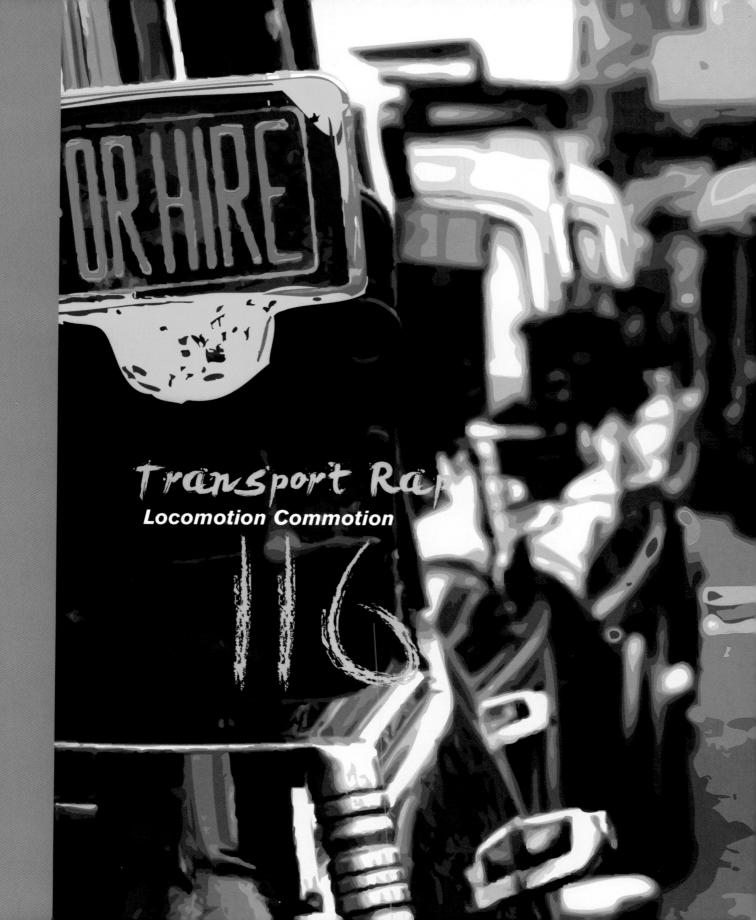

Transport Rap
Locomotion Commotion

Serial Celebration
A Matter of Faiths

142

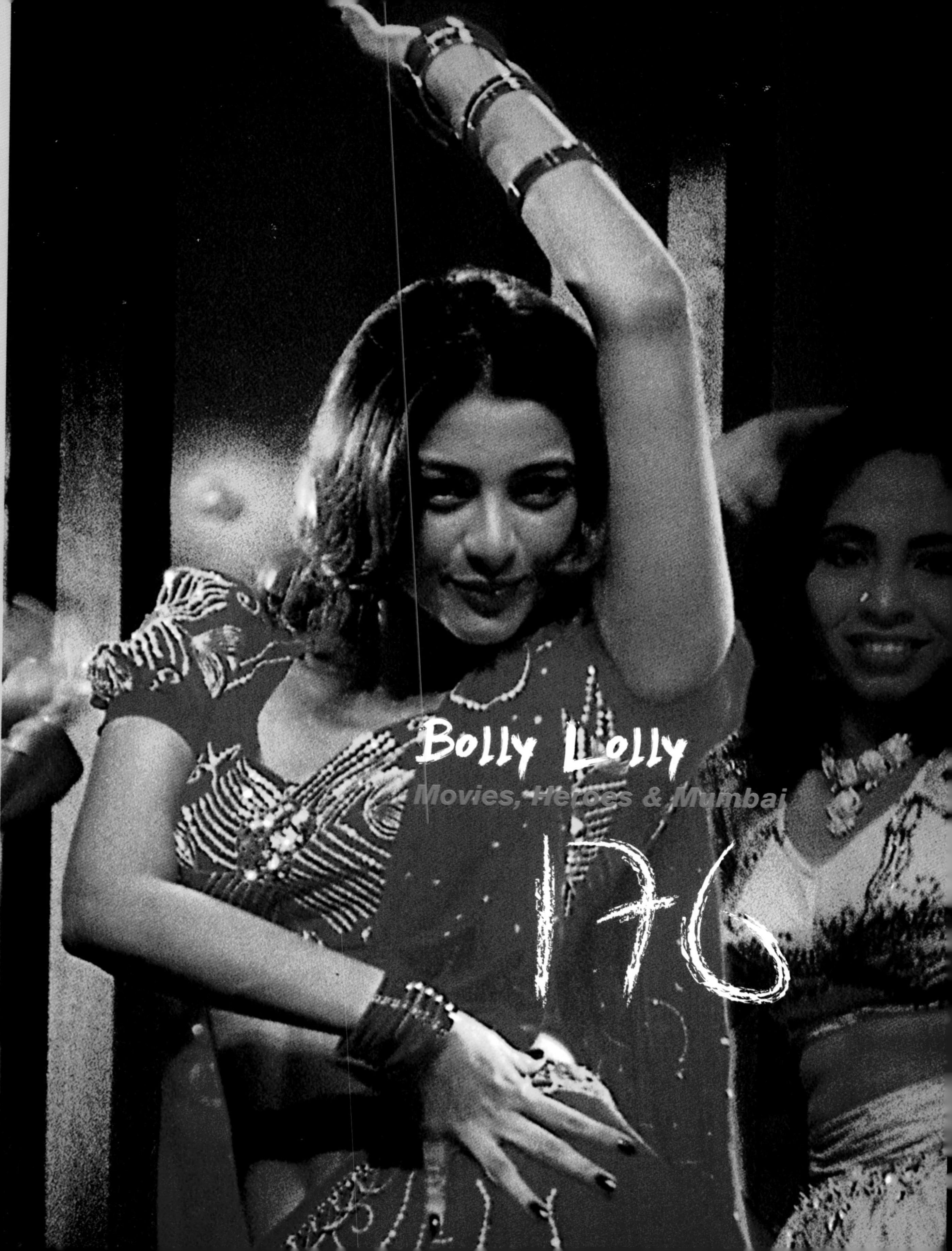
Bolly Lolly
Movies, Heroes & Mumbai
176

In an age where 'City' books are hitting us from all sides, and the visuals we breathe are laden with typical urban images, it came as a perfect opportunity for me to give back, on my own terms, to this wonderful city that has seen me grow as a person and a designer. It is a city that sustains me, breathes life into me day after day, every single day that I spend here. It supplies me with images continually, images that are glaring in their contrasts. The cliché 'city of dreams' is something you come to realize once you have lived in Bombay. The dabbawalla, the bai, the pandu, the baniya and the bhajiawalla all come together to form this city, hand in hand with the movers and shakers. As visual director, I have aspired for the graphics to breathe energy into the lesser noticed facets of the city. The mad growth and pace is seen in this art-meets-design book. A quirky take on a quirky city. It was conceived over many evenings spent observing the underbelly of the city. It led to many introspections about the

krsna mehta's

way we live. The collage that this complex city forms took shape in my graphics instinctively. It expresses the many layers we come across in our everyday dealings in Bombay. The paisleys and the patterns, the squiggles and the dots in my graphics all come together to bring to the forefront the positive energy this city exudes. Many photo-artists have documented the disparity and the poverty of the city. I have simply strived to bring forth its happy and celebratory nature. Where else do you see such a myriad of images? The immersion of the colossal idols in the Arabian Sea as a backdrop to Sushi dining? The coming together of various people from all walks of life? Where else do the people form the structure and the backbone of the city? Which other city moves on, despite all odds. I couldn't help but celebrate this spirit through a medium I knew best – Art. Do partake in the visual splendour that we call Mumbai Masti! Like someone once said, "Come to Bombay, come to Bombay, Bombay meri hai!"

foreword >>>

Mumbai Unzipped

EDGE: Enviable. Desirable. Greedy. Extravagant. Mumbai is all these. And has a lot of masti, fun, being so.

Like every city on the sea, it looks outwards and ahead – walking the edge of tomorrow, cashing in on today, living life as if there were no yesterday. And laughing all the while. That's what makes Mumbai.

Bombay-Mumbai – each of its names has symbolized these porous borders of time. `Mumbai' has gracefully leapt from past to present. It stems from the resident deity, 'Mumba Devi', who was worshipped by the original Koli inhabitants when the place was just a cluster of huts and fishing nets strung along an obscure shore. Reinstated after almost 300 years of being 'Bombay', 'Mumbai' is today equally comfortable as the zip code of a soaring megalopolis.

'Bombay' has an even more intriguing double identity. Colonial and free India alike waved it as their proudest pennant of enterprise. Expunged by chauvinist decree, 'Bombay' ceased to exist in 1995, but it has refused to die. 'SoBo' still stands for South Bombay, and its sophisticates refuse to abandon the earlier hey-day name. For them, `Mumbai' reeks of regressive provincialism. 'Bombay' exudes cosmopolitan cool; it is the amalgam of heady success and cheeky style, a combo which has been the city's signature for over three centuries.

"Bom Bahia! What a beautiful bay!" gasped Francis Almeida, the Portuguese adventurer who, in 1508, had arrived here, like so many fellow Europeans, in search of the fabulous riches ensconced in a peppercorn.

Charles II of England was less impressed by this marshy outpost when it was packed into the dowry chest of his bride, the Infanta of Portugal. Seeing that he could not turn it to quick profit, the king hived it off to the East India Company with speed and without sentimentality. He thus unwittingly laid the foundation of the typical Bombay deal. No gain? Drop without pain.

What gives Bombay its edge? Why is it envied and desirable, greedy and extravagant? It is just the way it was made.

The conquering powers contributed much more than its name. Port of call for thinker,

Massed Appeal. Mumbai offers experiences as multitudinous as the grains of sand on its famous beaches. No surprise, for this is a city of many parts, each of them as intriguing as the whole to which they add their might. The sea itself is the abiding leitmotif, chief player and silent observer of the tumultuous flow of people and events.

Taylor, soldier, sailor, enriched imperialist and lesser thief, Bombay learnt the tricks of all. Then, from this heady cauldron, it churned for itself a street-smart power greater than the sum of its borrowed parts.

Eyes fixed on the horizon, back turned on the grubby hinterland, Bombay has always taken full advantage of its location on the boundless sea. It has boldly imported the world's influences; then, using these to expand its mind and market cap, it has exported its global savvy with equal panache. Bombay was, and remains, an entrepot, not just for the exchange of commodities, but for the commerce of cultures; a stevedore to ambition as much as to the ocean liners it once serviced.

Like the sea, its godmother, it is ceaseless. Never hanging up the 'CLOSED' sign; it is always open for business, pleasure, and the sudden deal. Mumbai never dreads the midnight knock, always assuming it must be that of opportunity. Or of friends wanting to sweep it off to an impromptu – and masti-ful – party till dawn.

It was always rigged up for adventure wherever trade winds carried its ships, always ready for the main chance in peace and war. In 1861, when America's Unionists and Secessionists battled over the extension of slavery, the rest of the West was deprived of the Deep South's cotton. Far, far away Bombay stepped into the breach, and thus were born the mills which spun gold for all those who came here, drawn by the factory siren's roar.

Over a century later, it made a killing from another distant war. With Beirut's belly-dancers and blackjack tables afire with real bombshells, rich Arabs had to find another hotspot. Bombay was ready, willing and able-bodied enough to muscle in. It built entire hotels for the white-robed rush, and, when these deluxe caravanserais ran out of rooms, it checked the visitors in for check-ups. Dedicated to every Arab ache and whim, the five-star hospital was born.

So was a whole new tourist season. The desert people did not want to see the Museum or the Zoo. Clutching on to their billowing djellabahs, their old wives and their new umbrellas, they exulted in the city's savage monsoon, turning out in regaled force to marvel over the rain coming down in sheets, and the 60-foot waves crashing on Marine Drive. Overnight, the city's most inconvenient season, when hotels fine-tuned the art of the fly swat, became the busiest and richest of times. In fact, this Beirut bonanza saved the very expensively built Oberoi Sheraton from becoming a white elephant, and converted it into a cash cow with gold-dust on its eyelids.

Yes, Bombay holds the patent on the know-how for turning business into a pleasure trip, and pleasure into big business. This is why every Indian city or obscure Smallsville seeks secondhand glamour via a shop called Bombay Photo Studio, Bombay Tailors or Bombay Café. These may be nothing more than a decrepit hole in a peeling wall, but the association transfigures them. Note the name. The SoBo snobs are right. 'Mumbai' just does not evoke the same magic.

The most honeyed B-trap is Bollywood. Nothing gives the city its sequined cachet more than its film industry. Without doubt, argument or WTO violations, this is the country's most famous export. Bollywood has taken the city's culture, landmarks and the 'Bambaiya' patois to every nook of India, and to each corner of a foreign field that forever worships the film idols of home.

Stick My Lips. These women marched – and spun, and sacrificed – for India's freedom. Their inheritors have seized their own independence. Part-time maid or full-time business achiever alike are a distinctive breed, working hard at their economic independence, and creaming off a higher social status than their sisters elsewhere. They can twiddle a martini glass with as much aplomb as they can smash glass ceilings.

The city is on the cutting-edge of glamour, wealth and underworld mafia. Dawood Ibrahim, the Don Corleone of South Asia, grew up on the city's gritty streets, and seized supremacy over gangland and gold-smuggling before seeking safety abroad.

Indeed, Mumbai may be very good at what it does, but it does the bad even better. It walks the ethical razor's edge, making a virtue of the seven deadly sins. Greed, spurred on by Envy, propels it to all that it Lusts after, including the Gluttony that masquerades as gourmet pursuits. The Violence of organized crime may have diminished with the ganglords having either fled or been eliminated, but Wrath could still end in gory death, as its residents fight over water, wives or right of way. What is glaringly absent is Sloth. Slow down in Bombay and you'll get overtaken – or need the undertaker.

Now look at this perverse edge differently. Everything that would be a despairing negative anywhere else notches up admiration here. Dharavi is Asia's largest slum, but instead of being a template for squalor, it is a model of small-scale industry, a behemoth of humming establishments churning out everything from trendy leather bags to timeless pappadoms. Or take its claustrophobic commuter network. Don't condemn these as subhuman cattle trains; consider their steamy experience as the furnace in which the citizens' steel is tempered. Why, even being stuck in the tailback of cars at so-called rush hour is a symbol of Having Arrived.

The exceptional calamity reveals this advantage even more than the quotidian burdens. The 1993 blasts, the Noah-grade deluge of 2005, and the explosions which ripped through the packed local trains at rush-hour the following year could arguably be denounced solely as manmade or civic-official-aggravated disasters, but instead they became shining manifestations of human fortitude and sacrifice.

Tranquil, tempestuous; buoying, wrecking; as cold as a shoulder, as warm as a smile. Like its nurturing sea, Bombay-Mumbai has always been a collation of contrasts, but with a common current carrying its varied constituents towards the same gleaming shore. The city will lash you with its differences, but if you swim with its sharks, snap with its crabs, or sing with its dolphins, you will find that the apparent disparity is united at the core.

What binds this diverse mass together is a common restless ambition. Everyone is in search of a personal El Dorado – even if this is only the name of a tacky condo in a distant suburb. Everyone adopts whichever course is needed to get to the goal. The movement is always forward, even if it means briefly stepping back. For a city on the sea, stagnancy is death.

Similarity and contrasts, in Mumbai, both are the real thing. As obvious as a giant billboard on a building, and sometimes as concealed as the peeling plaster behind it. The most clichéd incongruity is the soar of skyscraper with the sprawl of slums at its feet. 'Om Shanti' is the chant of the haves as they pray to become have-mores.

Bombay Or Mumbai? Bombay sprang from the spontaneous exclamation of Francis Almeida. "Bom Bahia, what a beautiful bay!" cried the Portuguese adventurer when he beheld it first in 1508. Anglicised by the British who acquired it as part of a royal dower in 1661, 'Bombay' stuck on for their entire rule, and 48 years thereafter. Mumbai, the original name of the main island of a seven-beaded archipelago, had always been used in the local vernaculars of Marathi and Gujarati; it became official in every tongue and postal address in 1995.

Bom-babe Or Mum-bai? A certain snobbery still continues to be attached to 'Bombay', the label of commercial and social savvy. It denotes downtown sophistication and cosmopolitan cool, as opposed to the odour of provincialism attached to 'Mumbai'. But not for long. A new generation, oblivious of Bombay's cachet, has embraced the new-old name without protest or prejudice. They have taken to 'Mumbai' like an office assistant to the 9.15 Fast — or a socialite to a caviared canapé.

'Home Shanty' is the mantra of the slum-dwellers grateful that they have even this rag-and-tin roof, and are spared the humiliation of living on the pavement, or on the road divider, or even in the entrails of an abandoned drainage pipe.

Now, politicians and their developer cronies want to turn Mumbai into a Gotham where only lofty towers gleam, and lowly squalor is banished out of sight. But it is not that easy, and not simply for the usual reasons of too little money and too many questions on human rights. It is more complicated than that. Because slums are not just a superficial sore, they are a part of this city's soul.

It is not just the fact that the penthouse parvenu need the shanty close at hand to house those who sweep their duplexes and drive their Jags. It is not just that kings and pawns must share the chessboard of commerce. The truth is that the flashiest Mumbai-ite has something of the slum inside. Its energy, its cohesiveness, its stink…

He needs this alter ego to survive here. It has something to do with the excess of ambition, the shortage of land, the disregard for the finer points of gracious living in the overriding desire to overtake your business rival, your gym-mate, or your favourite beauty-salon sniper. In a dog-eat-dog city, bitchiness and mongrel manners are also zipped into the chic survival-kit.

Bombay flaunts its westernization with the same pizzazz with which its charmed habitués flash their designer labels and their frequent-flyer smiles. Trendy fashion lands here first, sartorial and semantic. Bombay wears and speaks the latest cool. In the room the women come and go, wearing Valentino and mouthing the newest lingo from *Vogue* and *Cosmo*. It was the first to learn the phrase 'walk the talk'. And the Bombabe talks it and walks it best. With buttered tones and toned butt.

Indeed, women are the litmus test of a city's liberalization, and those of Mumbai are as true-blue as it gets. Yes, Calcutta's sterling companies had Anglo-Indian secretaries in pencil-skirts long before anyone else. But in sober Indian terms, and not as a hangover of the Raj, Bombay produced the first cadre of white-lace-collar working women, a confident trickle that soon grew into the aggressive flood which pours out of and into the commuter caverns of CST and Churchgate every peak hour.

But contrast is part of its script, remember? So, for all its westernization, Mumbai is also tribal at heart. One artery may throb for everything that makes this a global capital, but the other thumps strongly for native roots. For those who live, love and masti-fy here, cosmopolitanism is their Corporate/Society identity, but community is their emotional glue. How can it be otherwise in a city made up of migrants?

Even if they don't live in the ethnic enclaves of Girgaum, Mohammedali Road, Kotachiwadi, Matunga or Dadar, they will make the pilgrimage there, occasionally or with metronomic regularity. They go to genuflect to family elders, to propitiate

ritualistic obligations, and most energetically to bow to the altar of their gastronomic delights. Khichda in Bohri Mohalla, patrel in Dadar Parsi Colony, bhakarwadi in Bhuleshwar, Amritsari fish which has now acquired the local branding of Koliwada… the list is as endless as the stream of migrants that makes up the demographic stew.

Indeed, migrants are Mumbai's main ingredient, its spice and garnish. They have made the city what it is: a be-there-or-be-dead kind of place. No fear. No mercy. Take no hostages.

Migrants have always poured into Bombay-Mumbai on a daily basis, in the kind of wave that countries reel under only in exceptional times of war or pestilence. They have to make it here because there's nothing left where they came from. But these neo-natives are not the usual soul-battered refugee. However miserable their previous life, their drive comes not from what they have left behind, but what they can look forward to. Migration here is Pull not Push. Everyone comes to Bombay in pursuit of a dream. Not just to wish upon a star, but to become one. And till that rich and famous time, breathing the same air as Supernova Amitabh Bachchan will do.

Its migrant karma shapes Mumbai in many ways. The 'de-domesticated' city needs to get every need serviced by an outsider. Whether it is sex in its globally infamous cages, or whether it is housing in a hostel, paying-guest, shared flat or stylish serviced apartment. It has created the phone-in lifestyle, and bachelorettes depend on delivery boys to a degree that gives their left-behind mothers a heart attack, and a complex. Phone the grocer for a tooth brush and ask the boy to pick up a beer on the way.

The incessant monsoon-pour of migrants affects everything, including the manic skyline and the insane infrastructure; concrete tenements rise and drainage crumbles due to the unrelenting inbound pressure. Migration has also created a Hindi so unlike the purist original that it qualifies as a separate dialect, 'Bambaiya'. Hindi, Gujarati, Marathi and so-called English collide like spermatozoa to impregnate this bastard Babel. The iconic phrase sums it up, 'We are like that only!'

But Bombay-Mumbai is like that only also because a common driver has always whipped this migrant maelstrom forward. Unrelenting, unflagging ambition propels this always-on-the-take, always-on-the-make city. The pan-Indian mantra of 'Please adjust' plays out differently here. It is not meant to make life less inconvenient; it is to make the climb faster. Pay off the cop not because you are too lazy to go through the legal process, but because you are too busy. A minute saved is a buck made. A moment squandered is a deal lost.

Delhi genuflects to political power. Till its recent apostasy, Kolkata sang hosannas to Maoist slogans. But Mumbai's resident goddess has always been 'rokda', cash, to be snatched with all ten arms. And with any artificial ones that are handy. Buck-creating business or 'dhandho' is the alpha and omega of its existence, cause and effect, the search and the fulfillment, the singer and the song. It is all-encompassing, taking every activity into its greedy embrace. To propitiate the omnipresent competitiveness, you need the gift of the grab.

This is why Bombay is as indiscriminate as a whore in the disbursal of its favours. Show me the money, and take the goods. Forget the foreplay. Here every kind of orgasm is fast, frenzied, 'fatafat'.

The commercial instinct is the basic instinct, and it plays out everywhere, from getting to work on those suburban trains to any other vehicle of Getting There. It shapes everything, from festive exuberance to communal rioting. Mumbai's most-feted deity is Ganesha, the god of entrepreneurial success, and his devotees are as secular as they are legion. Similarly, the horrendous blood-letting of 1992-93 came to a halt for reasons which were more commercial than humane. Muslims worked in Hindu-owned factories. Violence and curfew prevented them from venturing out of their ghettos and into the territory of the 'Other'. Production and profits plummeted. Good business sense prevailed.

Bombay's edge is also its acronym. It invokes envy and desirability in outsiders, and provokes greed and extravagance in those who have seized it as their home. The migrant mentality, its ambition, its restiveness, its need for constant reinforcement continues to chisel Bombay the way its shoreline continues to be contoured by the sea.

Ambition erodes the complacence of those who have settled down like its rocks: every new wave adds to the force that sharpens the competition, and threatens to turn the Arrived into the Also-rans. Every new wannabe has the potential to turn the queen bee into a has-been. Nothing can be taken for granted. The Marxian view of capitalism may never be cited in this corporate HQ of materialism, but success here as certainly 'carries within it the seeds of its own destruction'. The deal is only as good as the next hand from the deck of cards; it is always avariciously eyed by the next band of card-sharpers.

Much of Bombay's bustling dockside activity has shifted to the satellite ports custom built for the new container leviathans. The hum of the cotton mills turned into their bitter swansong after the fatal trade-union strike of 1982. Wealth now belches out of the smokeless industries of finance, IT, entertainment and fashion. The sprawling low-rise of the mill enclaves, once the throbbing heart of indigenous culture, are turning into an expensive, but soulless, Legoland, with commercial and residential spires spiking the skyline in an architectural electrocardiogram.

In the last 15 years, much has become slicker. But two basics remain. The board outside the small eatery still announces, 'Rice Plate Ready'; the placard on the dhobi's cart still says, 'Iron Ready'. The local word used for 'ready' is 'chalu', which also means smooth, as in 'smooth operator'. Appropriate. In this city's grab-as-grab-must survival stakes, you have to be chalu.

Like its midwife, the sea, Bombay has had rough weather which often rode in on winds of benign change. The reforms process of 1992 opened up all industry to competition. It was a good thing and a bad thing. Like adolescence, it gave business barons great freedom, but they had to give up their childhood protections. Like adolescents, industry wanted to explore the world, but didn't want the world and its Dad barging into its private room. Since all Indian companies of any consequence were based here, this petulant cartel came to be called the Bombay Club.

This wasn't the only way in which liberalization impacted it negatively. Bombay's urban supremacy reeled under the suddenly opened-up Indian economy. There it had been, lording it as City No 1, when, as overnight as an illegal tenement, all kinds of upstarts began muscling into its penthouse positioning.

Back Alley, But No Blues. The gleaming megalopolis has a seedy side. Never mind. It's a city that specializes in wresting success out of squalor, the silver lining is often more noticeable than the cloud. Slums are a beehive of entrepreneurial activity, and tumble-down tenements a real-estate opportunity. As Mumbai goes through yet another persona change to become a global financial hub, the detritus of its dock and textile days will soon disappear under the bulldozer.

The first threat to its Numero Uno status came from outsourcing which changed Bangalore from a dull 'Pensioners' Paradise' into a keyed-up 'Silicon Plateau'. Delhi, which had long basked in its languourous, Lutyens-bungalow lifestyle, converted an adjacent village into a chaotic Manhattan in a bid for the IT pie. Behind its deceptive jasmine chaplets and crisp dhotis, Chennai metamorphosed into a less flashy, but more stable, version of Bangalore. Hyderabad, long suspended in feudal formaldehyde, sprang to life as Cyberabad, the capital of not Andhra Pradesh, but 'Chandra Pradesh', thus named after its totally wired Chief Minister, Chandrababu Naidu.

Suddenly, not just the big cities, but every sleepy town was on Prozac, giving a wake-up call to the complacent mistress of the metropolitan manor. The barbarians arrived at the gates and stormed the once impregnable bastion.

From these alarm bells, a new resolve was born. True, some jumped ship, and swam to the lush new islands of IT-enabled opportunity. But the vast majority of Mumbai's hoary fighters pressured the civic authority to clean up its act and storm-water drains. Thus, again in typical fashion, the city turned threat into opportunity.

Besides, it already had a war-chest, the first-mover advantage. It was the original signatory of the MOU with global business, and more so with global attitudes and style. Everyone else was an arriviste, a wannabe. It had skyscrapers, business centres, fashion shows, discos, a Japanese restaurant long before anyone else. In short, it had unilaterally seized liberalization while the rest of India was still straitjacketed in restraining socialism.

This head start is far from being lost. However seductively the upstarts beckon with neon winks, however flashily they proclaim their mall-to-mall carpeting, for most Indians, Mumbai is still highest on the scale of objects of desire – with higher high-rise and, more alluringly, higher high-life.

Glamour is the new power. And its once and future peak is here. Nothing epitomizes this as much as the Page Three Phenomenon. It began as the party page of the *Bombay Times*, *The Times of India*'s lifestyle daily supplement introduced on October 1, 1994. It has grown into a social thesis, and has altered aspirations, gender equations, even newspaper consumption patterns.

It created a social genre, P3P, Page Three People, a frontal upper caste whose every move and cleavage flaunt gets documented in the public's eager consciousness. P3Ps began to oust the traditional Page One People with such vigour that the latter scrambled to become the former. Ergo, Delhi's political class, traditionally a slouch in the sartorial and social departments, suddenly became the last of the big swingers. And they began `airdashing' to Mumbai on quite another brand of party business.

Yes, this glitzopolis is the brand leader in The Party As Event, a new business opportunity which requires Harvard-grade management skills, and which has created a satellite system of ancillary industries. Money and glamour, 21st-century Mumbai has surgically enhanced the twin assets which had kept Bombay at the top of the league during the 19th and 20th.

Page Three created the Fishbowl Set, a social A-list whose entire existence is determined by the camera. But Page Three is only a culmination, a hothouse version of another defining feature of Bombay: show-biz. Bollywood (and now television production houses) may be the city's main attraction as well as its most lucrative commercial, but every Mumbai-ite, from the humblest upwards, is also always on show.

This is remarkably a city of publicly lived lives. The whole teeming megapolis is the 'samnewali khidkee', the 'opposite window' immortalized in the hit-song from the Hindi film, 'Padosan' or Neighbouring Woman. You won't always see the `piece-of-the-moon face' described by the rapturous lyricist, but a piece of the mundane action is always on view.

This open-to-public lifestyle may be unacceptable and unnerving in cultures with higher privacy quotients, but here it is a pedestrian occurrence. Literally so, because the street is the centre of the Bombay universe.

For those whose home is pavement or slum, the carriageway is front parlour and bedroom, kitchen and bathroom, even a nursery with babies sleeping blissfully in hammocks slung between parked trucks. The shanty-dweller migrant may conceivably move out of the street, but the street will never move out of him. It will continue to be his marketplace, for everything from dusters to dreams. Here he will grab a snack or get a job. Here he will buy a ticket to time-pass entertainment. Or become the unwilling object of it, like the lovelorn who, in this cramped city, have only the park bench and the sea-parapet for their romancing.

Voyeurism is as endemic to the city as deal-making. On the suburban train, you steal a glance at someone else's hand of cards. Men leer into the Ladies' compartment through the wire netting, provided ironically to ensure their safety. 'Ladies' commuters watch other women spilling out the minutiae of their lives like the contents of the handbag jolted off a polyester lap. With equal nonchalance, they chop beans for dinner or lay bare their domestic bogeys.

And when they all go home, they have no option but to stare through the actual 'saamnewali khidkee' of the neighbouring building, so close that they can pluck out their neighbour's life without overstretching themselves.

There is no escape from watching or being watched; everyone is co-opted into this 'peer' group. The old, closely packed tenements and fancier towers were built for staring into. Every new flyover opens up the inner vista of the apartment blocks that flank it. Sixth-floor seclusion overnight becomes the public domain of every passing vehicle. Private lives and crockery patterns are thrust upon strangers in an interlock of instant intimacy.

It cannot be otherwise. For a city on the edge, inside and outside are distinctions without a difference. In a migrant commune, there are no outsiders simply because there are no authentic insiders. So, the mantra of live and let stare should occasion no surprise. We've got the look.

Mumbai is not only like that. It likes it too. It's all part of the masti.

What are you, Mumbai? Who are you, Bombay?

City of a hundred thousand faces, and yet so often as faceless as an abandoned mask. Rich bitch or neither, which front would it care to pick today? Will it ever reveal its true identity? And, even then, how will we know it's the real McPatil? That it's not lying through its orthodontist-fixed smile? Again.

Mumbai is the dancer of the seven veils, or of 70. Look around. What you see may not be what you get, but you can be sure that what you do find behind the façade will be intriguing. The hoarding which proclaims the life hedonistic conceals a building patched with damp. The glitzy cinema poster is plastered on a tenement of flaking hope. Walk past a wall of crumbling brick and forgotten paint. Save your snooty disdain. Within this squalid exterior, millions of rupees may be made in a day. Or in an hour. Or lost with the same insouciance. No time-waste on regret. For the dealer inside knows that the Bombay pack of cards never runs out of aces. In the long run. And till that fortunate turn, there's always the Joker to tide you over the bad times.

Which Mumbai do you choose? Or, more to the point, which Mumbai chooses you as it swivels its seductive hips around you? The Western images on Indian walls are as much its trademark as the paan-stains. Is Coke the real thing, or is it aam-ka-panna, the tart, sweet juice of the raw mango? The latter's contradictions are also what Mumbai is all about.

Build a stylish apartment block, landscape it with Japanese gardens, embellish its façade with intricate patterns in mosaic or futuristic polyester film. Return to find that the residents have added their own design element which overwhelms all your intimate detailing – the saris and dhotis flapping nonchalantly in the afternoon breeze. Soaking in the sun, like old people on a wintered lawn.

The topography is a totem of the way life is lived here. Seashore, hills and claustrophobic inner cities are all symbols of its social formulae. The metropolis is as expansive as the beaches of Girgaum Chowpatty, Dadar or Juhu, open to the salubrious breezes and influences of the West. Spared both the hotheadedness and the coldheartedness of more extreme Indian parts, Mumbai is moderate in temperament and in temperatures; there is no summer of mayhem or winter of discontent.

The hills, Malabar, Cumballa and Pali, are the stereotypes of high living; of the crest of success that corporate achiever and social climber work at. Inner cities? Their clichés are the city's karma too, brutal warrens with people packed like rats in a lab experiment on overcrowding. Only this is no lab. This, also, is the real Bombay, as much in its spheres of razzmatazz as ragtag.

True. Very true. But in this city of perverse chimeras, the opposite is equally true. The beaches are not just balmy getaways or expensive sea views from socialite windows. The sands are littered with the flotsam and jetsam of the tide of humanity that washes up on Mumbai's shore. Lovers seeking the privacy of the rocks could find instead the kiss of threat. Once, smuggled gold, and later, the deadly RDX perforce chose more distant beaches on which to land before making their clandestine journeys into the city, but the shadowy stretches on the edge of glamour have areas of darkness, figurative and real.

The same is true of heights many feet above sea level. Antop Hill is the social antonym of Pali, Malabar and Cumballa. But people at the bottom of the economic pile also live on the top of all these addresses, the swanky ones as much as the non. Their tenements cling precariously to the side, and often crumble into swift extinction, swept away in the landslides of monsoon fury.

Inner cities defy the supercilious assumptions as cheekily. From the churn of this teeming, seething ocean is extracted the elixir of mortal hope, the Mahabharata's cosmic myth suitably adapted for our ungodly times. It's not just the humming hutment industry of Dharavi, every slum has sequins in its dirt. As with the beaches, both literally and metaphorically. And now the shanty town has glittering money too, as developers offer filthy lucre to turn its bubbling gutters into real-estate gold.

Mumbai, the dancer swirls its veils. Now you see its beauty, now you don't. Now you see its blemishes, now they're airbrushed over. It's that way from first sight. Other cities ease you into their ugliness. Mumbai delights in rubbing your nose in its squalor before it reveals its glamour.

Kolkata offers you a rural idyll when you come by train, and almost the same greenery even if you fly in. The migrant, arriving in Mumbai with stars in his eyes, and nothing more in his pocket than a dog-eared picture of a film star, is confronted with the backs of scabrous buildings lining the railway track, with their exposed drainpipes and sad plants struggling out of rusty cooking-oil tins.

The air traveller fares little better, and the one who comes via the international airport, ironically, does worse. The gleaming spires of corporate Mumbai shimmer on to the scene when he has almost given up hope, and would have turned around and returned to where he came from had the crazy snarl of traffic so permitted.

Settle into the city, and you won't know it better. Live there a lifetime, and it can still surprise you. You think it is all purse-strings, and, in its darkest hours, it becomes all heartstrings. Play on it like a violin, and it will make you weep. In the brittle laughter of its socialites you can hear the softly falling tears. Of gratitude from the recipient of a good deed quietly done. Or proclaimed unabashedly. Yes, Mumbai is in your face, more often than it turns its back on trumpeting. Publi-city is its second name. Tena-city its third. Auda-city its fourth.

Mega

Urbane

Manic

Bindaas

Arrogant

Individualistic

Mumbai flaunts each of its contradictions. With feli-city. And sometimes menda-city.

That's the masti of Mumbai. Fun, no?

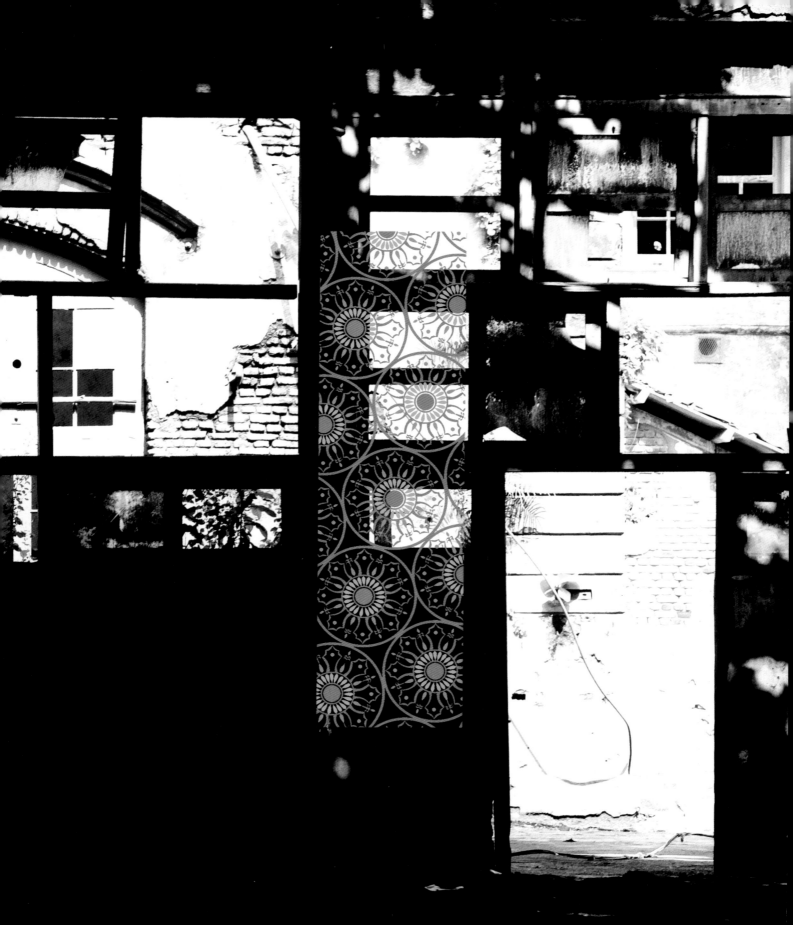

59

Location: Hotel Sahara Star, Mumbai

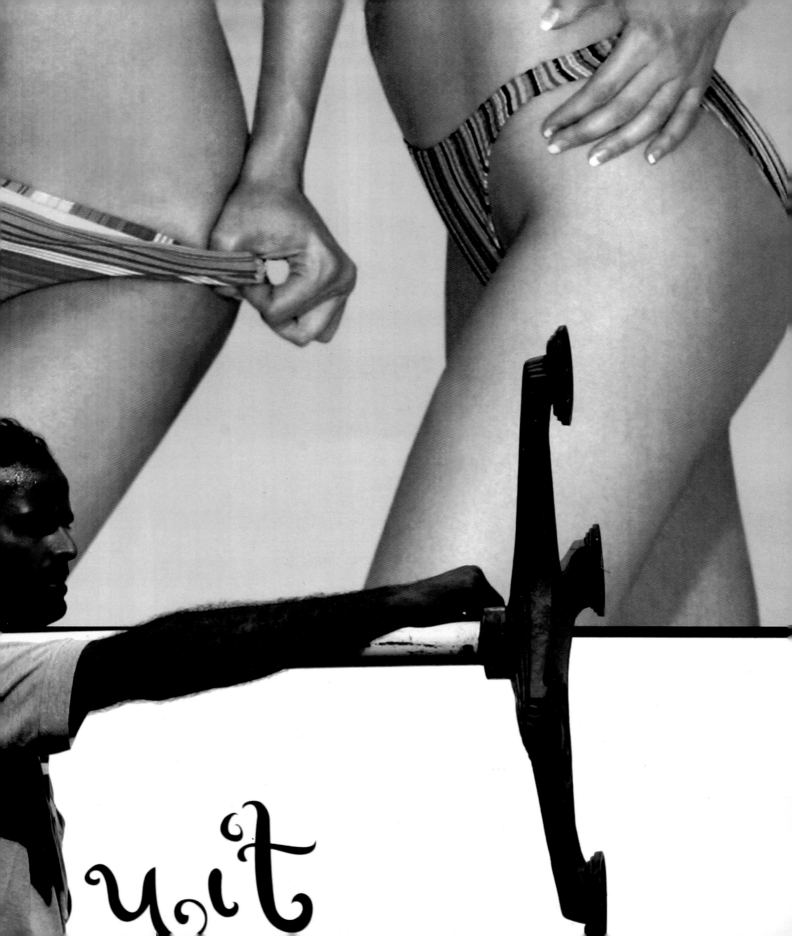

The Way We

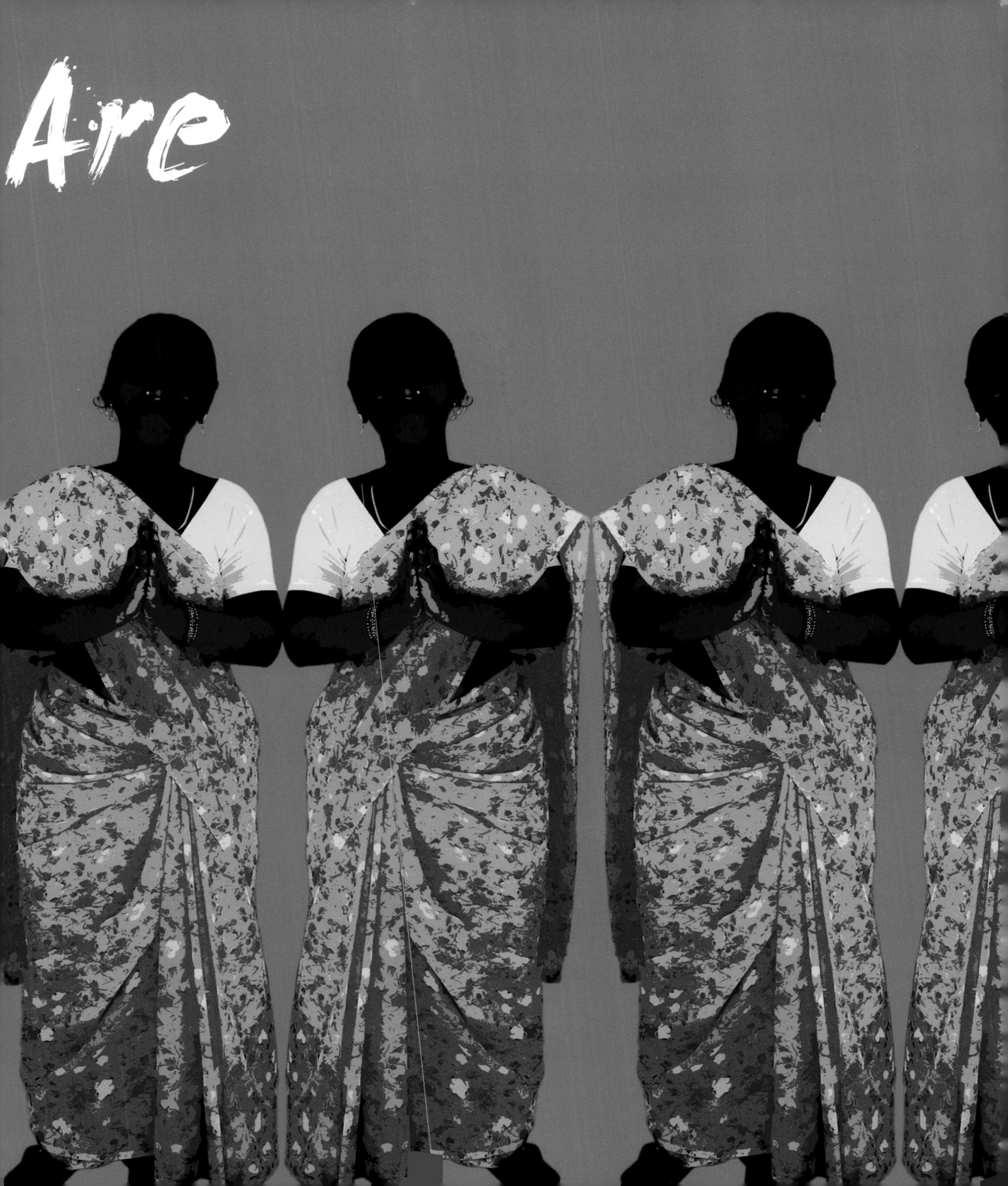
Are

Bombayites have to be street-smart because the street defines their existence. Life here is a public thoroughfare, with avenues of opportunity, potholes of frustration. The traffic lights are programmed for Go, seldom for Stop, and almost never for ambivalent Amber.

Nothing dominates the street as much as commerce. It has to since Bombay's birth, growth and successive reincarnations all stemmed from this imperative. The city makes the country's biggest bucks and fills the nation's coffers in the same proportions. The city is home to the richest Indians. It contributes 40 per cent of all income-tax, 60 per cent of all customs duty and 20 per cent of all central excise tax collections. But Mumbai's place in the accounts ledger of history is assured as much from the collective force of the millions of transactions struck on its greedy streets.

Here, more palpably than in the plush expanse of mercantile towers, you will see in action the city's primeval force: dhandho. This word comes from the Gujaratis, a community that is perennially in transaction mode. It has a subtext far more complex than its literal meaning. It is much more than 'business'; it is edged with the varied layers of a deal, as sharp as a business suit, as loaded as an extortionist's threat. You will bump into this omnipresent, omniscient fellow, 'dhandho', with every step you take on the Mumbai street.

Town planners and the terminally foolish may believe that pavements are for pedestrians, but those less out of touch with reality know that they are for hawkers. There have been many attempts to confine this intrepid species to designated markets. They may, on occasion,

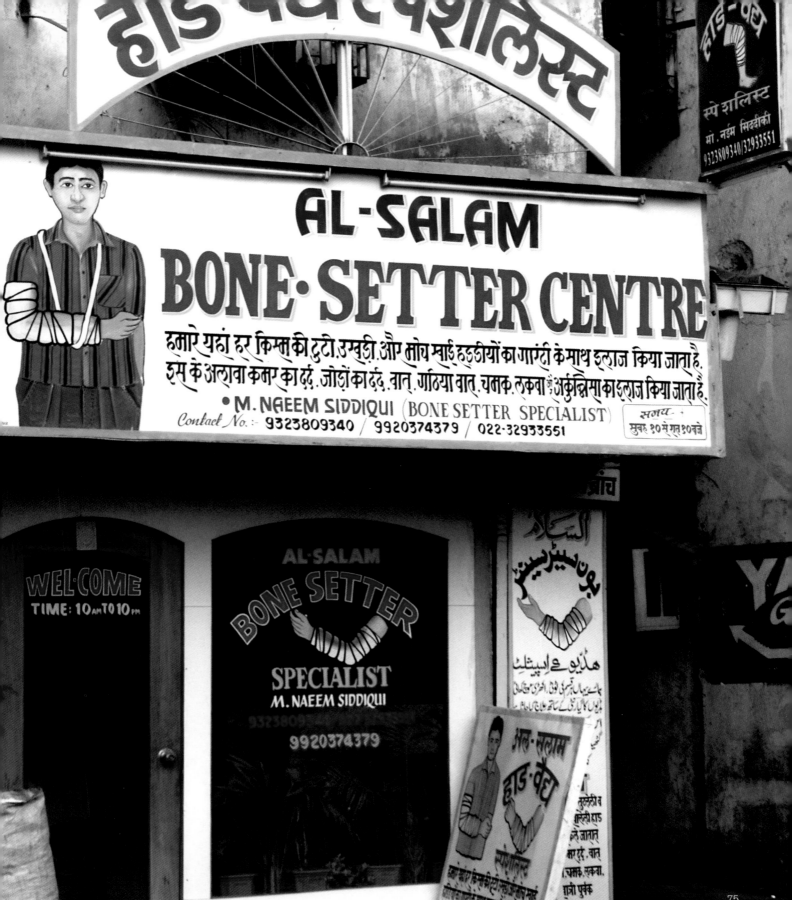

be successfully evicted, but the cleared space is soon colonized by the next bunch of migrants who came, and stayed on to pile them with peddled merchandise.

Mumbai may now be reconciled to the Writing on the Mall, but its most enthusiastic footfalls are still reserved for pounding the pavement bazaar. Anything you need, from a Lacoste shirt (fake) to a jasmine chaplet (fragrant), is available here at bargain price – with the added attraction of being able to whittle it down some more.

More than anyone else, hawkers practise the city's mantra of 'Encroachment is my birthright'. Colonizing the pavement, they push pedestrians off it. In their more assertive domains, they take over the carriageway itself. Except when the bush telegraph warns them about the imminent arrival of the municipal van ordered to cart them away, and they flee in a flurry of trays and cartons.

This is not the only avenue of street-level commerce. An entire economic system flourishes at the traffic lights. Peddlers of pirated books and secondhand bouquets, whining beggars, clapping eunuchs, perky street children wiping your windshield or trying to sell you a tabloid, with an irresistible song-and-jig routine. A meal, a baby's medicine, an addict's fix must all be earned in the 120 seconds it takes for the lights to change from red to green.

The street is a roster of Bombay's moving assembly line. Dabbawallas run with long trays of tiffin carriers perched expertly on their heads. Porters run to load and unload crates. The fishwife trots with a swivel of monster hips to balance her stink-dripping basket. Streetwalkers stand to solicit custom in the noonday blaze. Yes, kerbside trading here is more than an activity of the Bombay Stock Exchange.

Stand, stare, run, walk, buy, and best of all, eat on the street. The Supreme Court and municipal health inspectors pass orders against roadside food which spreads Bombay belly, but Bombay's fired-up bellies are served well and variously by the zillions of shops, stalls, stands and carts on every by-lane and street corner. Indeed, food is the totem of a migrant city. All its multiple flavours mix and rise from the hissing griddles on its streets. Like this hungry megapolis, the food supply never sleeps.

Like the street on which it is sold, the bhelpuri provides its own metaphor of the city. Like life here, it is spicy, sweet and tangy. Like Bombay's business, it is mixed together with speed and efficiency from a ready set of ingredients. Like pleasure here, it is instant and satisfying. Like its demography, it is easy to tell one component from the other, but they combine into an integrated whole, tastier than each separate part.

Or consider Pav Bhaji, a love child, born in the alley with an indeterminate paternity and a smother of butter. Its genes are Maharashtrian, Gujarati, Punjabi, Sindhi, and more than a dash of *je ne sais pas*. Goan pav-bread wades into this spicy mash of vegetables. It is likely to be cooled off with a kulfi, dispensed from the earthen pot of an as-earthy 'bhaiyya' from the Indian heartland. Or washed down by a localized hot 'n' sour soup from the adjacent 'Chinese' cart, manned by a high cheek-boned and pale-skinned youth who has fled the mountains of his native Garhwal or Nepal to explore the life exciting in magnetic Bombay.

Yes, each newcomer may dip his spoon into Bombay's soup kitchen, but he also adds a shake of his own to pepper up the communal stew.

Time Never Stands Still In The City That Never Sleeps. Mumbai is always fully wound up, fully charged. There's no bigger arena to watch this than the street, even when it is only the alley along which you crawl. You can buy anything you need, and don't, on the pavements. Which is why it might seem that these were laid for hawkers, not pedestrians

Clocking Life. The street is the new arrival's first stop; here he sets up his house and the business with which to support his family. When he moves out, he continues to eat or find entertainment here. Migrants pour into Mumbai at the rate of 300 families a day, though the rise of other urban centres has somewhat diverted this surge.

Brushstrokes Of Hope. The humblest lane exudes the hues of aspiration and disillusionment, triumph and despair. Literally too, the country's best known and most controversial artist, M F Husain, started life in a Muslim alley here and made his early living as a painter of cinema hoardings. He was one of the six founder members of the Progressive Artists' Group which, in 1947, established India's contemporary art movement and nurtured almost every painter and sculptor of note.

Porter House Rules. The entire country moves through Mumbai's long-distance stations, mainly CST and Mumbai Central.

Runaway Success. The unlettered dabbawalla is now a Harvard Business School wow. One-time peasants, using nothing more than a code of symbols and their unflagging feet, carry thousands of hot lunch boxes (dabbas) across the far-flung city via a complicated relay system without ever delivering a fish curry to a vegetarian office-goer. Recognition of their skills has come in forms as varied as Six Sigma certification and an invitation to the second wedding of Prince Charles.

Fried, Ride and Tried. Anything goes in Mumbai. Or comes. No other Indian city offers such a pastiche of cultures, experiences, sights or sounds. Anybody can, and does, arrive here in search of hope – and finds it. Even those whose home is nothing more than a paste-up of rags and ragged cardboard still manage to shrug away their squalor, and swagger into the sunset with the typical Bombay version of attitude. A street meal of fritters is savoured as much as a platter of five-star foie gras. A sybaritic ride in a snazzy 'Victoria' down Marine Drive could be followed by a crowded suburban train ride home.

Walking The Razor's Edge. It's a cut-throat place, and most of those who have finally Arrived got here by a close shave. The barber at the street corner will offer to give you the style of your favourite film 'hero', but the result is likely to resemble the original as much as a Bollywood plot resembles reality. Equally, the city's growing band of 'coiffure artistes' has become almost as famous as the stars for whom they create cuts at hair-raising prices.

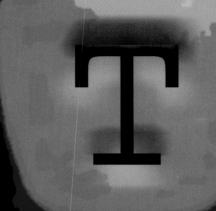

E

T

Key To Success. Name it, we'll provide it, from a mundane job application hammered out on a battered roadside typewriter to a frivolity of glass bangles that tinkle out an aria of flirtation. The city has the uncanny knack of converting the prosaic into the poetic. And does the reverse with even greater efficiency.

C

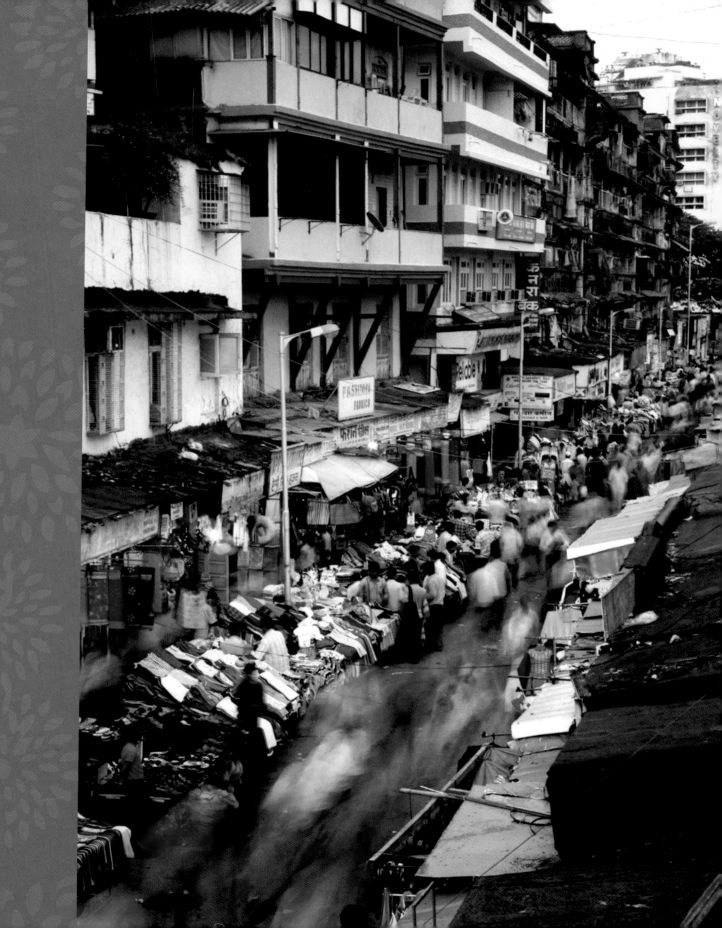

It's A Fishmarket Out There. Mumbai's origins are still visible in the teeming Sassoon docks and other markets, even if hi-tech trawlers have scaled up the exercise, and coastal cuisine has become the *au courant* dining experience. For all its boasted sophistication, Bombay is a bazaar not a boutique, any which way you look at it. Metaphorically, and more so physically, with massive, dedicated marts for everything from flowers to faucets.

The Frame-Up. Hardware and antiques are the stock-in-trade of Chor Bazaar or Thieves' Market which scatters the paraphernalia of an abandoned past along the smelly, serpentine bylanes of the Muslim quarter. You are unlikely to discover a rare masterpiece, but hope can still be found amidst the junk.

The Café Society. Here it has different connotations and different components. 'Leo's' is a Colaba Causeway landmark that made the planet less lonely for backpackers long before it was granted immortality in 'Shantaram', the incredible autobiography of a global drug-runner who briefly became a Mumbai slum-dweller. The Irani café, with its distinctive bentwood chairs, round marble-topped tables and cantankerous owner at the cash counter, is a Bombay special, but alas giving way to sanitized, deodorized, but utterly soulless, fast food parlours.

की टोपी

● मुंबई टाइम्स टीम

'रत पिया को छिन बिसू...
अशी विविध रागदारीत...
संगीतबद्ध केलेल्या वा. रे...
अवीट गोडीच्या रसाळ गा...
तरुण गायकाने सर्वांपुढे...
देशपांडे यांच्या गा...
वारस गवसल्याची खात्रीच ...
प्रसिद्ध नाटककार विज...
शब्दबद्ध केली. 'नाटवाच्या...
संचारलेले इथे आपण पाहतो...
आड यायचं नाही', असे उद्ग...
समस्त रसिकांना आपल्याच...
साक्षात्कार झाला.

पं. वसंतराव देशपांडे यांना आदरां...
सभागृहात झालेल्या 'वसंत उत्सव' या...
दिवस हा राहुल देशपांडे स्मरणीय ठरवला. आ...
तीच फिरत, तशाच पहाडी आवाजातल्या ताना, आलाप
आणि तालाला घट्ट पकडून डौलात कोणत्याही रागात संचार
करण्याची त्याची हिंमत याने सारेच भारावून गेले. आजच्या
तरुणांमध्ये पं. वसंतरावांच्या कलमारग्री गायकी पहा...

ला नाना

...च्या भूमिगत वावरणाऱ्या
...रिसकांना झाल...
...त अनौपचारिकपणे
...संवाद साधला.
...श्वेश्वर इथे झालेल्या
...साध केली होती,
...रून गेली. नानाने
...खजात हा किस्सा
...काही वर्षांनी
...शस्तीची आठवणही
...ऐकून अ पली प्राज्ञ
...य, याची जाणीव होते.
...नाना नसते, तर एवढा
...नसता, असं राहुलनेही
...ते आवर्जून सांगितलं. कुमार
...या भेरवीने सांगता झाली.

असा प्रश्न अनेकांना पडतो. नाट्यसंगीत,
...शी यांचा कितीही खजिना असला, तरी त्याआधारे
आसपासच्या स्पर्धा, मैफलींमध्ये आपली मोहर कशी
उमटणार, याची अनेकांना भ्रांती असू शकते. पण त्या...
...राही तमा न बाळगता या तरुणाने जी तयारी आप...

गायकीत गायवला,
गंधर्वांच्या अवधूता या भैरवात त्या...
सांगता केली. महाराष्ट्र टाइम्स या...
पार्टनर होतं.

मैफलीत वसंतरावांच्या आठवणी
कातरून ती आपल्या डोक्याव...
बोलावणारे आणि पहिल्या रांगेतल्या
मिश्किल शैलीत पर्दाफाश करणारे
आठवले. तर पंजाब घराण्यातला रंग
घराण्यातल्या श्रेष्ठ गाणं आपल्या...
गायकीतलं कसब पं. अशोक
दाखवलं. रानडे यांनी वसंतरावांच्या...
मांडल्या. त्यांचं श्रेष्ठत्व संगीतानं...
आपली ...य वाढणार आहे का, ...
त्यांनी ...रणाबद्दल ...
...या पत्ररूपी ...

Location: Hotel Sahara Star, Mumbai

Tea For Two. The chai shop is iconic all over India, but here it is not political barometer or matrimonial match-fixer. Here it is a business stoker. Typical is the 'cutting chai', the shared cup or glass which reflects the city's tightfistedness as much as its open-ended camaraderie. The penny-pinching trader even has a subtle sign-system that indicates to the peon whether the tea he has 'hospitably' ordered for the client should in fact arrive, or be delayed till the fellow gets fed up and departs.

PALMIST FOR YOU
JUPITER
SATURN
SUN
WILL
LOGIC
LOVE
MARS
HEAD LINE
HEART LINE
LIFE LINE
LUCK LINE
MARS
VENUS
MOON
BRACELET

A Money-Splendoured Thing.

'Rokda', cash, and 'dhandho', business are the city's currency, its driver, its adrenalin. The Sensex of the Bombay Stock Exchange is the major index of the country's corporate health. It was established in 1875, and its address bluntly proclaims its business; Dalal Street translates into Broker Boulevard. Mighty though the Sensex may be, the literal 'kerbside deal' is no less powerful, or less cunning. In the claustrophobic warrens of the historic commodities markets millions of rupees worth of transactions are made on the basis of a mere word or simply a primeval sign language. Money cannot but be the resident deity of a city that was born in greed, which grew to alluring womanhood on the seductions of commerce, and now seeks global nirvana as a financial hub.

Transport Rap

No horn, OK, thank you please.
Take a ride. Be taken for a ride.
Whichever means you take
Be sure you have Arrived.

> Move ahead please. Make room please.
> Give side please.

All aboard the autorickshaw, or the cab, train or bus.
Choose what you will,
You'll get the Transport Rap.

> The bus conductor thinks he's Hitler.
> The cabbie thinks he's Schumacher.
> The auto guy thinks he is Alpha and a Romeo.
> But the train driver only wants to get you to the office on time.

Curse them, thank them, can't do without them,
Whichever way you look at them,
You're in the Transport Rap.

> You're in the Slow train even in the Fast train.
> Take a taxi if in a hurry, but get stuck in a jam.
> The auto says he'll get you there with time to spare.
> But his wheel may well roll off, and the clutch's beyond repair.
> Doesn't matter, doesn't matter,
> Jaldi karo, mister.
> Can't you see I'm speeding, sister.
> In this city you go places if you really don't care
> How you get there.

Locomotion, circumlocution, difficult location
No Entry, No Left Turn. No Thoroughfare.
No way to avoid the Transport Rap.

> Red Means Stop
> And Green Means Go?
> Bakwas, rubbish, you are talking, no?
> Is this your Baap ka rasta –
> Your father's road.? Or did you get it in your dowry?
> Chalo, chalo, aage chalo.
> Get a move on, Hero,
> Or I'll fix you.

Pothole, No Parking,
Signal jumped, Show your licence
        Pay a fine. Okay, bribe will do.
                They call it chai-pani,
                    Just some 'tea and water' to quench a traffic cop's thirst.
Give, give, take take, get on with your work.
          Who wants the jhanjhat-messing
Of a day in court.

Jostling, squeezing, sweating, belching,
Bombay-Mumbai is always on the move.
            The bus queue is orderly only till the bus arrives
              But, truth be told, unlike Delhi's killers,
Our red monster has a heart of gold.
Check it out, baby,
          When the flood waters take their toll.

The Slow train stops at all stations
         The Fast train stops between them.
It's a cattle-wagon inside
            In which may well hide
The milk of human kindness.
        The cab driver dreams of the girl he's left behind
              The auto-chap will return the purse you left behind.

However unlikely it might seem
There's a code of the road
Which is why there's no problem with
The Transport Rap.

The swanky car door opens
              And the fat cat inside puffs his cheek, pouts his mouth
            And spews out betel juice – and abuse if
                You dare to protest. Yes it's a test
To be driving in Mumbai. Oh yeah?
Try walking.

But even with that you won't avoid
The Transport Rap.

Run or get run over.
This is Bombay, my love. Shove it
To the Transport Rap

चर्चगेट
चर्चगेट
CHURCH GATE

535

4

535C

Track Record. Almost 2.2 billion is the combined population of China and India. It is also the number of people who shake rattle and roll, jostle, trample, and sing hymns in chorus on Mumbai's suburban trains every year. The Central and Western network is truly the city's lifeline. The city's vaunted commerce would wheeze to a halt if people could not commute from their far-flung suburbs, and surge out every morning like a tidal wave from its two business district railheads. The trains are as much about life as about lifelines. They are Mumbai in microcosm. Packed. Public. Brutal. But, throbbingly, touchingly, bondingly human. Push, push, thank you, ma'am, there's always room for one more behind on the seat of the 9.15 Fast.

Rush hour is crush hour. The historic and architecturally awesome Victoria Terminus now bears the name of the legendary 17th-century Maratha warrior-king, Chhatrapati Shivaji. Riding the loca

in demands the same agility, tenacity and audacity with which he wrested his empire in mountainous terrain. Grab a cab.

Auto Eroticism. Three-wheelers are free-wheelers, a law unto themselves, the bane of motorists, pedestrians and their own petrified passengers alike as they weave manically through the congestion. 'Pay by Meter' says the legend on their dashboard. That's if it's working, has been 'downed' at the start of the journey, or is not 'jumping' more crazily than the ramshackle contraption. Autos are allowed only in designated suburbs. Good for orderly traffic. Bad for those who want a cheaper-than-a-cab-if-not-as-private ride.

Take A Stand. Like the New York cabbie, Mumbai's taxi driver is the quintessential philosopher-cynic. He will give you an opinion on life, love, municipal politics and the box-office chances of the latest hyped movie as he negotiates monster potholes, exchanges pleasantries with a passing kinsman, and chuckles as he squeezes other vehicles into the road divider. No charge for all these extras. Just sink into his over-the top velvet upholstery, breathe in his incense, and relax, while trying to keep your mind off his driving. That's if he has agreed to take you on board in the first place. As often, it's a case of 'Wherever you're going, I'm not going your way.' You want to go south, he wants to go west; you want to get to your appointment; he wants to get to his lunch. As heartless as helpful, he will drive past without a sideward look when you try to flag him down in pouring rain. And splatter you with slush in the bargain.

MH-01
L8547

Mitsubishi.

With consecutive Dakar victories from 2001 to 2007, Mitsubishi is indeed toda... ...uted leader in performance ...chine is built to handle th...

MH-01
L8547

3.2MP Cam...

Wi-Fi...

View/Edit...

moments like those speak

MH-01
L8547

बेस्ट

MH-01
L8547

SAFETY IS OUR MOTTO

DO NOT TOUCH LEFFT CUT ITEMS

DO NOT LEAVE ANY BAGGAGE BEHIND.

No Butter For The Jam. The red monster of the road is surly, burly and not at all subtle in its belief that might is right. The conductor will ring the bell, the driver will start, well, with a start, and the wannabe passenger will have lost his foothold on the footboard. But compared to the buses of other Indian cities, the BEST service lives up to its acronym. It doesn't kill like Delhi's Blue Line, and it isn't a tin of sardines like everywhere else.

If it's Tuesday it must be Ganesha puja. Wednesday is for the Novena at Mahim Church. On Thursdays, Hindu women fast for Vishnu as they do on Mondays for Shiva, and Saturday's for the monkey-god Hanuman. Friday is namaz day at the mosque. Sunday, of course, is open house for faith dealers of every dispensation. This devotion is not just a 'week-ness'; Mumbai's calendar has a festival a month, if not three. Setting the celebratory tone for the rest of the year, January has been known to host both the ritual sacrifices of Bakr-i-Id and the ritual kite-flying of Makar Sankranti, with homage to the flag on Republic Day included for secular measure. Mumbai may be a city that worships Mammon, but God is certainly in his heaven.

However, celebration rather than faith is the operative word; the fervour is more in the expression than in the belief. This also explains why you don't have to be Hindu to immerse yourself in the festivity of Ganeshotsav. Or Christian to join the throngs which choke Bandra during the Mount Mary fair. Or, be a Muslim who has fasted all day to partake of the delicacies of Mohammedali Road during the holy month of Ramzan.

'Bombay' undoubtedly 'multi'-fied the monoculture of Koli 'Mumbai', but the original fishing village netted many influences long before the European cultural invasion. The Buddhist Mauryan and Hindu Satavahana, Shaka, Rashtrakuta and Chalukya dynasties established their settlers from other parts of India from the 4th century BC to the 8th AD. The expanding Delhi Sultanate led to the capture of the island of Mahim by the Muslim ruler of Gujarat in 1348; the area's many mosques and dargah festivals still stand as testimony to history.

Christianity may have landed further down the coast with St Thomas in Kerala, but trade and religion make easy co-travellers. Thus, Mumbai had these influences long before Almeida entered its harbour, changing its name and character forever with his spontaneous exclamation. After they forced the Sultan of Gujarat to cede the Mumbai archipelago in 1534, the devoutly Catholic Portuguese converted the locals. Protestant missionaries got into the act when Bombay moved across the chessboard of maritime power, and England established its long sway. But the Catholics had been there first, and today's DaCosta will accost-a you to assert this.

Bombay's community pot was, however, enriched much more by the continuing Hindu-Muslim tug of domination; strife seems to have been a booster for the city's growth right from the start. The Maratha challenge to the fading Mughals in the early 19th century created such instability in western India that merchants and artisans fled to Bombay for safety. Over the decades, Hindu Jains and Muslim Bohras and Kutchi Memons repaid their refuge dues in ample measure.

Among the new migrants were the Zoroastrian Parsis who came from their Gujarat villages and flowered into the city's most influential community. Indeed, different generations of one family, the Wadias, laid the foundation of Bombay's two defining industries, shipbuilding and textiles. Urbane, middle class and insular, Parsi festivals are private, but their unusual features and ways mark them out as the city's most distinctive minority.

Nearly two centuries later, the Hindu-Muslim fundamental upsurge of the 1990s seeded Bombay with an unfamiliar religious belligerence. But monochromatic bigotry can never thrive in a city shaped by the rainbow coalition of migration – or one where the primary hue is commerce. Thus, uniquely in Mumbai, the whole kaleidoscope of Indian festivity livens up the urbanscape, while never holding up the fundamental business of buck-worship.

Little wonder then that Mumbai's most native, most effusive and most secular festival, is that of the elephant-headed Ganesha or Ganapati. No celestial member of the Hindu pantheon is more lovable or allows such artistic licence in portrayal, but neither of these is the real reason for Ganesha's popularity here. He is the god of auspicious beginnings, and no venture, small or mall-sized, can be launched without his blessings. Naturally, he is the presiding deity of a city whose chief devotion is to mercantile enterprise. 'Dhandho' makes the perfect consort of Ganesha.

During its similar mass-celebration of Durga Puja, Kolkata completely shuts down, but during Mumbai's 11-day-long Ganeshotsav, festivity and brisk business happily co-exist. Bazaars and snack stalls flourish especially in the old mill enclaves of Lalbaug and Parel which metamorphose into a fantasy world of fairy lights and gaudy pandals, housing giant idols of the elephant god.

The one day that the city does come to a standstill is when the idols are immersed. Monster lorries accompanied by frenetic throngs – and seemingly the entire police force – slowly bear the beloved Ganesha through the streets, to the sea, and thence back to his heavenly abode. The air is heavy with clouds of sacred gulal, shouts of 'Ganpati Bappa Morya, Return Soon the Following Year', and the frenzy of dancers exploding to hysterical drumbeats.

No Full Stops For Celebration — and the commerce thereof. The market is the obligatory consort of religion, and ad hoc stalls mushroom under the benign rain of festival-time. Garlands and coconuts for the deity, the paraphernalia of ritual, and, as always in the seamless coexistence of the secular and the sacred, balloons for your son and ribbons for your own little goddess.

Five Chillies And A Lemon. This is the foolproof antidote to whatever evil or envy your enemies expose you to. These potent combos are sold at street corners every Saturday, and hang from everywhere, from rusty autorickshaw bumpers to designer doorways.

The Name Is Band. Frenetic drumming makes religious celebration palpably more so. It sets the beat and pace for a typical 'Bambaiya dance' which, like so much else in this city, was born on the street, and knows no other home. Called the 'rhumba-samba', it may be Latin – or double Dutch – to the original practitioners of these genres, but this highly energetic expression is the obligatory accompaniment to virtually every religious procession.

Heads, You Lose. Effigies of the ten-headed Ravana, abductor of the virtuous Sita in the epic Ramayana, are ceremonially set on fire in a symbolic triumph of good over evil. Lord Rama fought a marathon battle with the lord of the demon asuras, defeating him on Dussehra, the 10th day. The other representation of this seminal conquest is the victory of the 10-armed Durga over Mahishasura, celebrated at the same time. The mother goddess is also worshipped in her manifestation as Amba Mata.

Indian miniature Classical Art of traditional min contemporary fe attention.

R. K. Sharm
"Krishna and

Goodbye To Ganesha. All of Mumbai turns out to bid farewell to its most loved – and most lovable – deity, Lord Ganesha. The god of auspicious beginnings and good fortune is a favourite all over India, but has a special niche in a city driven on the adrenalin of 'dhandho' or the business deal. However, the origin of this mass celebration was political. During the freedom struggle, Maharashtrian leader Lokmanya Tilak turned family worship into a community festival as a means of forging a national Indian identity.

Passage To Heaven. Ganesh takes the sea-route home. Over the decades, certain Ganapati 'mandals' have acquired truly celestial stature. The 'Lalbaug cha Raja' is neither the tallest nor the most ornate idol, but 'he' is the crowned king of the festival. His immersion procession takes over 12 hours – from its pandal in what is otherwise a fish market in the old working class ghetto of Lalbaug to the sea. Millions have lined up in queues almost two kilometres long during the festival, and many more wait to pay him final homage. Like some others, Lalbaug cha Raja is a 'wish-fulfilling' idol.

At The Cross Roads. The Christians of Mumbai constitute their own melting pot – or salad bowl. Let alone the denominationally different Protestants or Syrian Christians, even the Catholic East Indians, Mangaloreans and Goans are distinctive in culture and dialect. Yet, they all share a zest for song, dance, food and the good life, collectively spicing Mumbai into a vindaloo. The East Indians trace their roots to the original inhabitants of Mumbai, and maintain their pre-Christian traditions and language.

A-Spiring To Divinity. A myriad churches bring character and diversity to the Bombay landscape. Christianity first came via Kerala, where St Thomas landed in 52 AD, but massive conversions occurred with the arrival of the Portuguese in the early 1500s, and to a lesser extent with the British, who may have established a far secular presence, but did not have the first-mover advantage in proselytizing.

BAI
PIROJBAI DADABHOY MANECKJI
VATCHA
AGIARY
Estd 19th May 1881

Minor But Major. Mumbai is home-base of the ethnically unique Parsi-Zoroastrian community. Now dwindled down to just 100,000 worldwide, they have been name-makers and visionaries in every field, including philanthropy. Winged Assyrian bulls flank some of their fire-temples, pointing to the 6,000-year-old roots of Zoroastrianism. Children are initiated into the faith in a Navjote ceremony, which has been influenced by this once-Persian community's 1,000-year-long Indian sojourn.

Salaam To Islam. Muslim communities here are diverse – Shia or Sunni, Dawoodi Bohra, Kutchi Memon, Ismaili Khoja, Baghdadi... Yet, they are quintessentially Mumbai. Their cuisines are clearly demarcated as are their individual niches in the ethnic enclave of Mohammedali Road.

Arabian Jewel. The Haji Ali mosque and tomb, 1431, of the merchant-saint is one of Mumbai's most visited shrines, even though the causeway that links it to the mainland can only be crossed at low tide. Pilgrims swell to 40,000 on Thursdays and Fridays, and like the dargah of Makhdoom Ali at Mahim, it is a secular following.

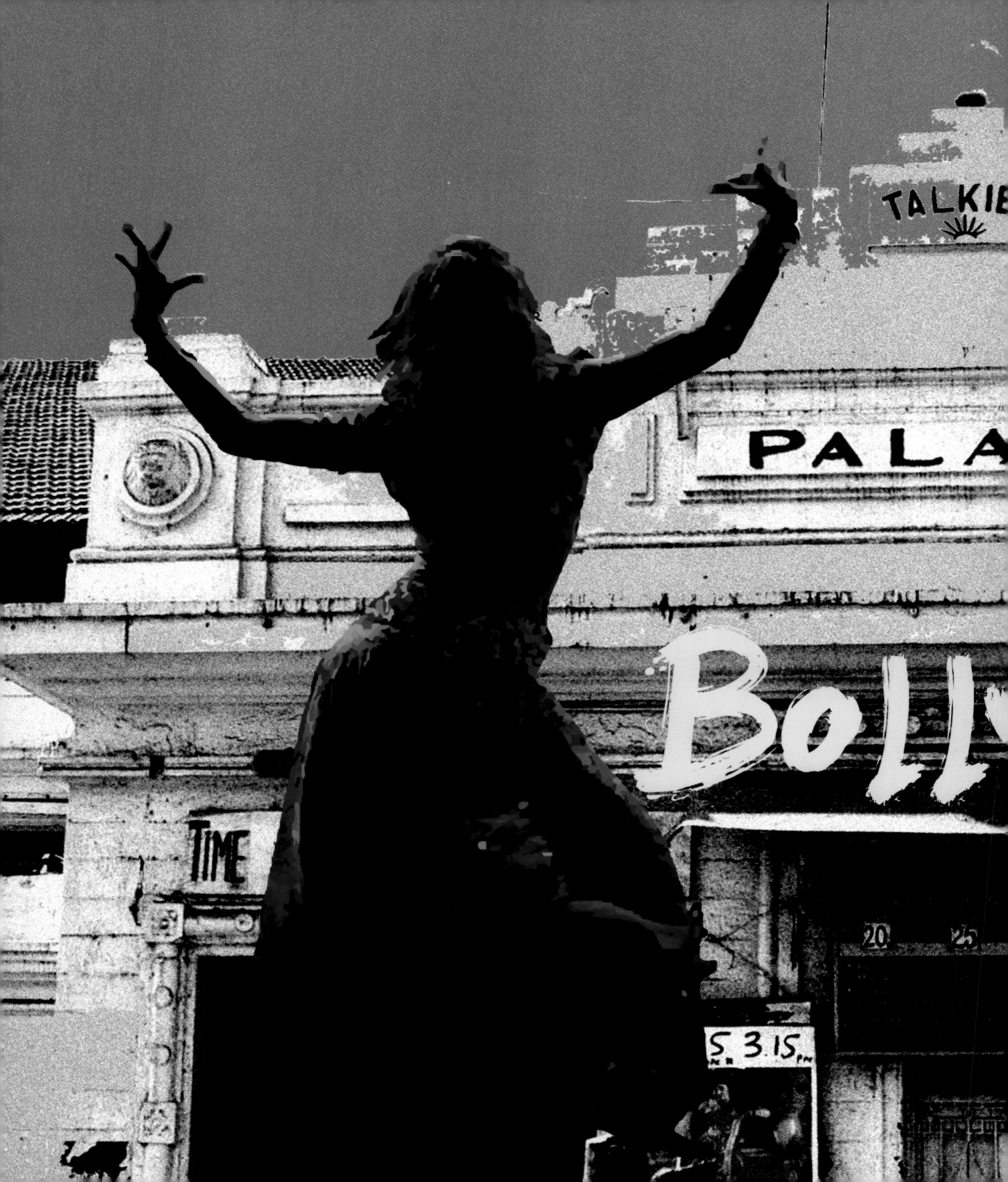
TALKIE
PALA
Boll
TIME
20
25
5.3.15

What plunged the entire country into a state of shock, and brought all normal life to a standstill? The assassinations of Mahatma, Indira or Rajiv Gandhi? The multiple terrorist attacks that ripped apart buildings, markets, buses, trains, and even the hallowed precincts of Parliament? Nah! Nothing rivalled the pan-Indian fan anguish that accompanied the two critical illnesses of the hyperstar Amitabh Bachchan, usually referred to simply as 'The Big B'.

Pujas were performed and Novenas offered for his speedy recovery. Women fasted. Men wept. Children flunked their tests because they were unable to concentrate on their books. Lovers stopped in mid-canoodle. The hitherto unheard-of ailments, 'myasthenia gravis' and 'diverticulitis', tripped off the tongues of toddlers as easily as 'Jack and Jill'. And the hospital spokesman became a national celebrity, basking in his two-and-a-half minutes of fame as television channels beamed 24x7 news bulletins on every detail of the idol's progress.

Welcome to the high-powered, hyped-up, hysterical world of Bollywood.

India's Hindi film industry gets its name from Bombay. And it had acquired such a life of its own that it couldn't conceivably have been changed to 'Mollywood' when the city became Mumbai. As rent, Bollywood has allowed the city to revel in its reflected glory. If the most obscure hamlet looks up to Bombay in admiration and envy, it is because this is the home of the stars.

Today, not just the lowly village but the whole world acknowledges that Bollywood is what makes India a global soft power. The streets of everywhere, from Toronto to Tasmania, are cleared to accommodate its location shooting. Conversely, gangs of leggy blondes high step in its chorus line in place of the earlier fat and tacky extras, or junior artistes as they were euphemistically called. And even Nicole Kidman danced to Mighty Bollywood's tune – literally – in her number in 'Moulin Rouge' which was inspired by a Hindi film hit.

City and industry share a symbiotic relationship, both feeding and feeding off each other. Certainly, they have become interchangeable in the popular imagination. If Bombay is India's most potent migrant magnet, it is not only because it offers the strongest chance to earn a living. It is because its streets are paved with stardust.

Every day, from every state across the country some adolescent or the other jumps on to a train heading in the general direction of Bombay with a film song on his lips and the flame of fame in her eyes. He may end up forever only on its cruel streets, she may end up in a worse predicament. However disappointed, the swagger never quite leaves their hearts. Just the notion of being in the home of the stars is enough.

Bollywood may not hold the original copyright on the magic of the movies, but it certainly has bought it over. Lock, stock and soft-focus. It can well afford to. It beats Mother Hollywood in terms of size; it is arguably the world's biggest film industry. Its worth in 2006-07 was pegged at USD 1.2 billion, its three top male stars command USD 3.7 million per film plus a percentage of profits, and it produces 150 movies on an average each year. In 2006, seven of these smashed the box-office as spectacularly as a villain's jaw.

Similarly, while all films across the world influence popular culture Bollywood has,

EROS
MUGHAL-E-AZAM
NOW IN COLOUR
RE-RECORDED IN
Dolby Digital
show timings:
2:45 pm
6:00 pm
9:15 pm
Sterling Investment Corporation
K. ASIF'S
MUGHAL-E-AZAM
Colour
music NAUSHAD
show timings:
2:45 pm
6:00 pm
9:15 pm
A Dinesh Gandhi and Boney Kapoor Release through Raksha Distributors.
4553

SUPER HIT, FAMILY DRAMA, LIFE KA SIDE-EFFECT, SHAKE YOUR BOOTY, GRAB YOUR LOOTIE, DHISHUM DHISHUM ACTION THRILLER. HERO. VILLAIN, ITEM NUMBER. YEH HAI BOLLYWOOD AND BAMBAI MERI JAAN.

PYAASA

MALA SINHA
GURU DUTT

MAHEDA KUMAR
JOHNY WALKER

by a long shot, panned into the Numero Uno trend-setter. This is not only because its catchment area is the one billion population of the Indian subcontinent plus the growing diaspora. That's a populous factor, and an important one. But the truth is that Bollywood goes into parts of the psyche that its peers don't reach.

It plays a lead role in everything Indian, from father-son relationships to real-life murders and heists to the age at which girls go in for boyfriends or Botox. 'Gymming' was in, and 'thunder thighs' were out as soon as heroines' legs stopped resembling the tree trunks they routinely danced around. It's not an exaggeration. The degree of defiance or docility, attitude or demureness, the angle of a local stud's swagger or the tautness of his abs are all determined by the latest blockbuster, the latest Hero No 1.

Yes, Bollywood – and by extension, Bombay – has made inroads into every segment of Indian life. It has shaped the lexicon. No, actually it has scrambled it into a 'baida ghotala' of the kind dished out from greasy griddles on the city's streets. It has taken its patois into Hindi's most purist domains, and even inveigled itself into territories which refuse to speak Hindi on the principle of cultural superiority.

This bastard language is Bambaiya, a Babel of Hindi, Urdu, Gujarati, Marathi and several phrases of indeterminate lineage. City and language are so melded together that it is no longer clear whether art imitates life, or vice versa. Do films speak 'Bombay Hindi' or has Bombay begun to speak 'film Hindi' – no one knows for sure. Or even gives a damn.

That's not all. Several, otherwise sane people speak entirely in dramatic Bollywood dialogue. Film lines become part of lingual legend. And mobile phone service providers, always the first to sniff out social spoors to convert into business opportunity, have entered into a joint venture with Bollywood. Wallpaper and similar merchandise apart, caller-tunes and ring-tones are no longer just the first bars of a song; phone someone, and expect to hear chunks of film dialogue while you wait.

Mumbai cashes in unapologetically on the cachet of its most celebrated tenant. Bombayites insouciantly accept the awed gaze of those less blessed with such proximity. For decades, Bollywood has acculturated the whole country to Bombay's landmarks, and chances are that an Indian is more familiar with Marine Drive than with parts of his own hometown. Bollywood has given Mumbai a Recognition Quotient that Hollywood certainly has not bestowed on LA.

There's more, much more. Thanks to the all-pervading influence of Bollywood, all Bombay has acquired the fantasy of a dream sequence, the sizzle of an 'item number', and the adrenalin of the fight to the finish. Dishy-dishy, dhishum-dhishum, Bombay's got it all. It has become the Big B.

But should we give reel-life all the credits? Perhaps the city was the real inspiration. Bollywood is not about subtle 'films', it's about in-your-face 'movies', right? It's not art auteur, but pure commercial, right? Hasn't Bombay been that way too – right from its opening shot? It set the formula of lusty life, love and laughter. Mast-mast masti has always been a must-must.

HOTEL
SHALIMAR
PALACE
2nd Floor
दिनेश पटेल का
दिव्यशक्ति
समीर मल्कन
नदीम श्रावण

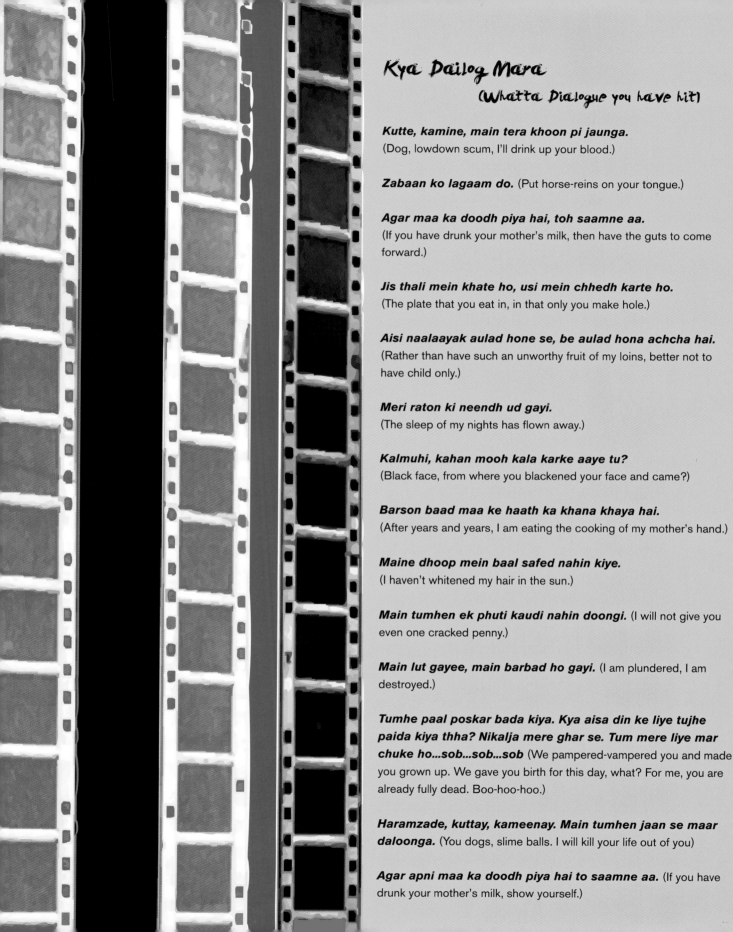

Kya Dailog Mara
(Whatta Dialogue you have hit)

Kutte, kamine, main tera khoon pi jaunga.
(Dog, lowdown scum, I'll drink up your blood.)

Zabaan ko lagaam do. (Put horse-reins on your tongue.)

Agar maa ka doodh piya hai, toh saamne aa.
(If you have drunk your mother's milk, then have the guts to come forward.)

Jis thali mein khate ho, usi mein chhedh karte ho.
(The plate that you eat in, in that only you make hole.)

Aisi naalaayak aulad hone se, be aulad hona achcha hai.
(Rather than have such an unworthy fruit of my loins, better not to have child only.)

Meri raton ki neendh ud gayi.
(The sleep of my nights has flown away.)

Kalmuhi, kahan mooh kala karke aaye tu?
(Black face, from where you blackened your face and came?)

Barson baad maa ke haath ka khana khaya hai.
(After years and years, I am eating the cooking of my mother's hand.)

Maine dhoop mein baal safed nahin kiye.
(I haven't whitened my hair in the sun.)

Main tumhen ek phuti kaudi nahin doongi. (I will not give you even one cracked penny.)

Main lut gayee, main barbad ho gayi. (I am plundered, I am destroyed.)

Tumhe paal poskar bada kiya. Kya aisa din ke liye tujhe paida kiya thha? Nikalja mere ghar se. Tum mere liye mar chuke ho…sob…sob…sob (We pampered-vampered you and made you grown up. We gave you birth for this day, what? For me, you are already fully dead. Boo-hoo-hoo.)

Haramzade, kuttay, kameenay. Main tumhen jaan se maar daloonga. (You dogs, slime balls. I will kill your life out of you)

Agar apni maa ka doodh piya hai to saamne aa. (If you have drunk your mother's milk, show yourself.)

Cash And Carry On. Films are the opiate of the masses – and the classes are even more addicted. For a long time they followed a fixed formula, set to scores of songs and five times as many costume changes. Some may have become a tad more realistic, but the vital escapism will never end up on the editing floor. Mumbai's old movie halls are architectural landmarks as well as pop pilgrim centres, though, alas, many have made way for the cookie-cutter multiplex.

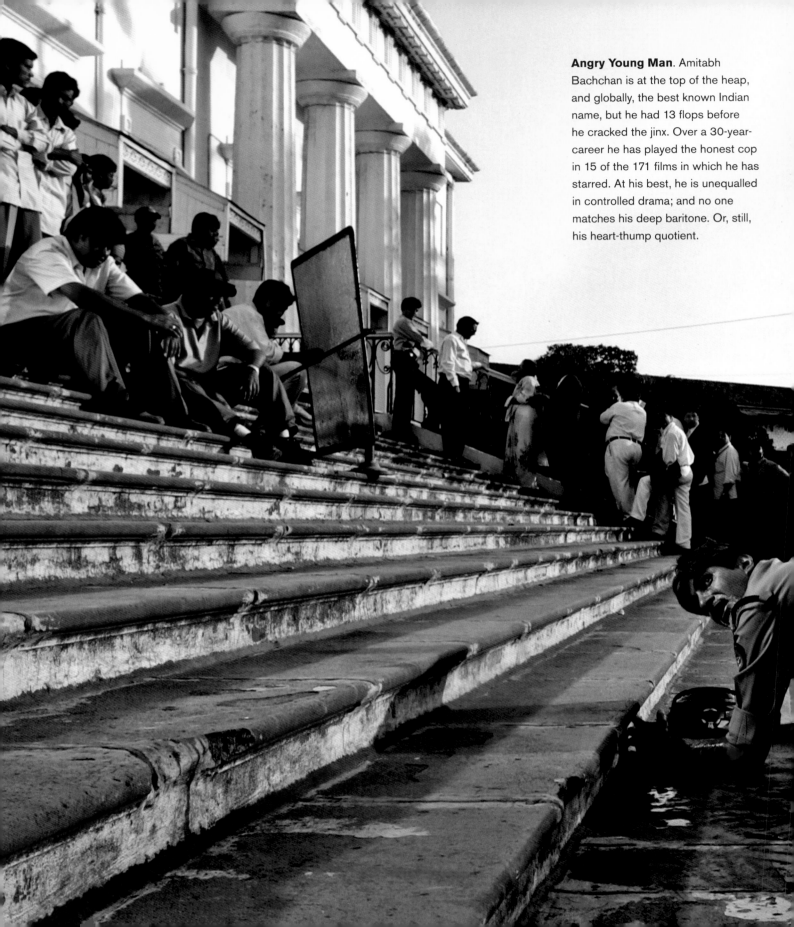

Angry Young Man. Amitabh Bachchan is at the top of the heap, and globally, the best known Indian name, but he had 13 flops before he cracked the jinx. Over a 30-year-career he has played the honest cop in 15 of the 171 films in which he has starred. At his best, he is unequalled in controlled drama; and no one matches his deep baritone. Or, still, his heart-thump quotient.

Poster-Script. Film hoardings will be inscribed with the names of the director, producer and lyricist, but never those of the actors. Stars are instantly recognized – and mobbed at every real-life appearance. Chennai has its Mollywood, Kolkata has its Tollywood, and Bangalore has recently come up with its own film industry, Sandalwood. But, for India, the planet – and all those watching out there – the only reigning movie mogul was, is and forever will be Bollywood.

TO NIGHT

TO-NIGHT

NARIMAN FILMS

DON

Produced By: Nariman Alrani   Directed By: Chandra Barot
Written By: Salim Javed   Music: Kalyanji Anandji

1975

EXCEL ENTERTAINMENT PRESENTS

A FILM BY FARHAN AKHTAR

DON

PRODUCED BY RITESH SIDHWANI

MUSIC SHANKAR EHSAAN LOY   LYRICS JAVED AKHTAR   DIRECTOR OF PHOTOGRAPHY MOHANAN

MULTILANGUAGE SUBTITLE

DVD
VIDEO

2006

PHOTO CREDITS

SARZ AGGARWAL